SAVE OUR ANIMALS!

Mountain Gorilla

Louise and Richard Spilsbury

Heinemann Library
Chicago, Illinois

Customer Service 888-454-2279

Visit our website at www.heinemannlibrary.com

Photo research by Hannah Taylor and Fiona Orbell
Designed by Michelle Lisseter and Ron Kamen
Printed in China, by South China Printing Co. Ltd.

10 09 08 07 06
10 9 8 7 6 5 4 3 2 1

Library of Congress Cataloging-in-Publication Data
Spilsbury, Louise.
Save the mountain gorilla / Louise and Richard Spilsbury.
    p. cm. -- (Save our animals!)
Includes bibliographical references and index.
ISBN-10: 1-4034-7808-2 (library binding-hardcover)   ISBN-10: 1-4034-7816-3 (pbk.)
    1. Gorilla--Juvenile literature. 2. Gorilla--Conservation--Juvenile
literature. I. Spilsbury, Richard, 1963- II. Title. III. Series.

QL737.P96S637 2006
599.884--dc22

                         2005028000

Acknowledgments
The author and publisher are grateful to the following for permission to reproduce copyright
material: Ardea pp. **4** top, **29** (Y Arthus-Betrand), **5** top left (J Rajput), **22**; Steve Bloom pp. **7**, **27**;
Corbis/ Reuters p. **18** (F O'Reilly); DFO p. **24**; Digital Vision pp. **5** middle, **6**; Empics/ AP Photo p. **26**
(R Ngowi); FLPA/ Minden Pictures pp. **13** (G Ellis), **21** (K Wothe); FLPA p. **28** (Silvestris Fotoservice);
Getty Images/ National Geographic p. **9** (M K Nichols); Naturepl.com pp. **4** bottom left
(M Carwardine), **11** (B Davidson), **15** (K Ammann), **19**; NHPA pp. **14** (J A Scott), **23**; Oxford
Scientific pp. **4** middle, **5** top right, **10**, **12** (A Plumptre), **17**; Reuters p. **16**; Still Pictures p. **5**
bottom; WWF-Canon p. **25** (M Harvey).

Cover photograph of mountain gorilla reproduced with permission of Digital Vision.

The publishers would like to thank Annette Lanjouw and Chris Loades at Fauna and Flora
International for their assistance in the preparation of this book.

Every effort has been made to contact copyright holders of any material reproduced in this
book. Any omissions will be rectified in subsequent printings if notice is given to the publisher.

Some words are shown in bold, **like this**. You can find out what they mean
by looking in the glossary.

Contents

Animals in Trouble

There are many different types, or **species**, of animals. Some species are in danger of becoming **extinct**. This means that all the animals from that species might die.

All the animals shown here are in danger of becoming extinct. These species need to be saved. The mountain gorilla is one of them.

The Mountain Gorilla

Mountain gorillas are the biggest gorillas in the world. A male mountain gorilla can weigh more than two people and is very strong.

Mountain gorillas live among the trees of the forest.

silver hairs on back

wide head

thick hair

Gorillas mostly walk on their hands and feet.

The mountain gorilla is an ape. This means it has no tail, a flat face, and a flat nose that points downwards.

Where Can You Find Mountain Gorillas?

You need to travel to three countries in **Africa** to find mountain gorillas. The countries are Uganda, Rwanda, and the Democratic Republic of Congo.

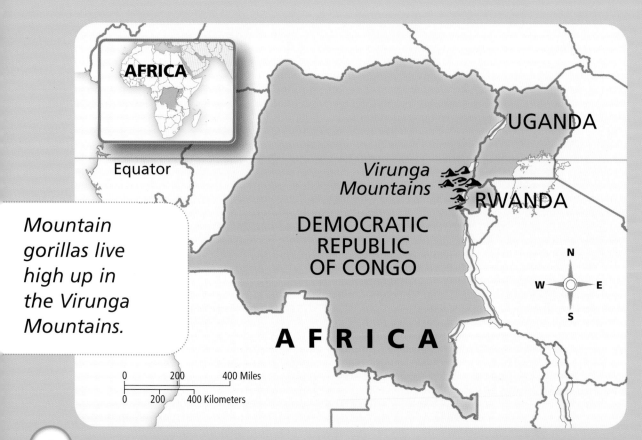

AFRICA

Equator

Virunga Mountains

UGANDA

RWANDA

DEMOCRATIC REPUBLIC OF CONGO

N
W E
S

A F R I C A

Mountain gorillas live high up in the Virunga Mountains.

0   200   400 Miles
0   200   400 Kilometers

Mountain gorillas live in thick forests where it can be very cold at night. The weather is usually cloudy and damp. This is the gorillas' **habitat**.

The mountain gorilla's thick hair keeps it warm.

What Do Mountain Gorillas Eat?

Mountain gorillas spend about eight hours a day eating. Gorillas are mainly **herbivores**, which means they eat plants.

Mountain gorillas eat for hours, then relax together.

Gorillas eat a lot of different types of plants.

Mountain gorillas have sharp teeth for biting through plants. They eat vines, thistles, ginger, and wild celery. They rip off the leaves with their huge hands.

Young Mountain Gorillas

This **female** gorilla feeds her baby with her milk. She feeds it until it is two years old. Then she teaches it which plants are safe to eat.

Like other **mammals**, baby mountain gorillas drink their mothers' milk.

The silverback protects the babies and females.

Mountain gorillas live in family groups. This big **male** gorilla is the leader. He is called the silverback because he has silvery hair on his back.

Natural Dangers

A mother gorilla keeps her baby close to her. If she leaves it alone, it could be in danger. Some wild animals kill baby mountain gorillas for food.

Leopards sometimes kill young mountain gorillas, so their mothers protect them.

Some people catch baby mountain gorillas. They sell the babies for a lot of money. Hunters usually kill the parents to catch a baby gorilla.

The baby gorilla on the left has been rescued from hunters.

Hunting Mountain Gorillas

In the past, hunters shot many adult mountain gorillas. Some people kept the gorillas to show that they were good at hunting.

Hunters sometimes killed gorillas to make **traditional** medicines.

These veterinarians are helping a mountain gorilla that got stuck in a trap.

Today hunters sometimes catch gorillas by accident. The gorillas get stuck in traps put down for other animals. A few people still hunt mountain gorillas for meat.

Dangers to the Mountain Gorilla's World

The biggest danger to mountain gorillas is that they will lose their **habitat**. People cut down trees because they need space to grow food.

When trees are cut down, gorillas have less space and less food.

Many people came to the Virunga
Mountains in 1994 to escape from
a war. They cut down a lot of trees
to build homes.

People in these
homes came to
the mountains
to be safe.

How Many Mountain Gorillas Are There?

No one knows how many mountain gorillas there were in the past. People only began to count gorillas in the 1950s.

Year

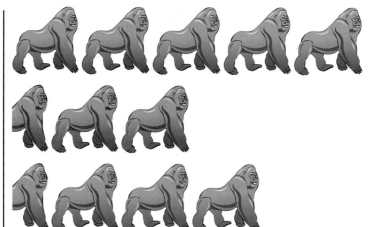

1958

1978

2004

 = 100

This graph shows that the number of gorillas is slowly growing.

Now people protect gorillas.
But gorilla numbers grow slowly.
A **female** gorilla only has three
or four babies in her life.

Female mountain gorillas only have one baby at a time.

How Are Mountain Gorillas Being Saved?

The mountains where the gorillas live are now a **national park**. Guards protect the gorillas and teach people to look after the forest.

These guards carry weapons to stop people from harming gorillas.

These guides are learning how to help the gorillas.

Guides take tourists to see the gorillas. If people get jobs as guides and guards, they will want to protect the gorillas even more.

Who Is Helping Mountain Gorillas?

Governments in **Africa** work with local people to protect gorillas and their **habitats**. **Charities** there and in many other countries also help.

The Dian Fossey Gorilla Fund works to learn more about gorillas and how to help them.

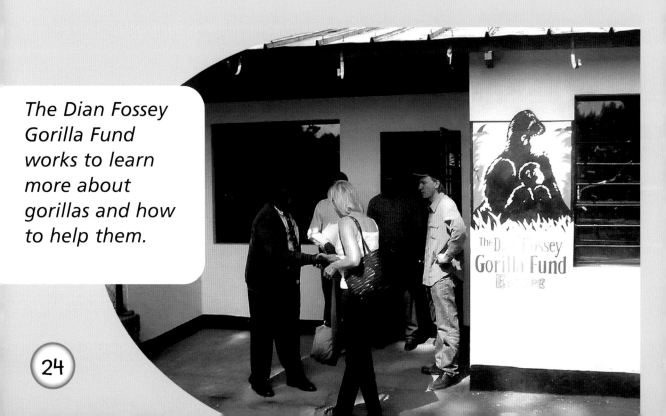

WWF is a charity that works to protect mountain gorillas. It teaches local people to live without destroying the forest.

People use photographs to help keep track of gorillas.

How Can You Help?

It is important for people to know that mountain gorillas are in danger. Then they can learn how to help save them.

If you learn all about mountain gorillas, then you can tell other people about them.

Here are some things you can do to help.

- Ask your school to adopt a mountain gorilla with the **WWF**.
- Join a charity that helps save gorillas, such as Fauna and Flora International.

The Future for Mountain Gorillas

Hopefully, there may be more mountain gorillas in the future. There are so few left today that they could become **extinct**.

Most people want to protect the mountain gorillas.

Let's all work to save these gorillas before it is too late.

There are laws to protect mountain gorillas. But some people still hunt them and cut down forests. These people need to learn how to live without harming gorillas.

Mountain Gorilla Facts

- Mountain gorillas sleep in nests. They make nests on the ground.
- Most mountain gorillas live in groups of about 10 gorillas. Some groups have over 30.
- Gorillas don't drink much. They get the water they need from the plants they eat.
- Every gorilla has a different set of fingerprints, just like humans do. Each gorilla also has different wrinkles on its nose!
- A silverback may be as strong as ten people.
- Gorillas live for about 40 to 45 years.

Find Out More

Spilsbury, Richard and Louise. *A Band of Gorillas*. Chicago: Heinemann Library, 2005.

Kendell, Patricia. *Gorillas in the Wild*. Chicago: Raintree, 2003.

Web Sites

To find out more about charities that help gorillas, visit their Web sites:

Fauna and Flora International: www.fauna-flora.org

WWF: www.worldwildlife.org

Glossary

Africa large continent. A continent is a large area of land divided into different countries.

charity group that collects money and gives help to animals or people in need

extinct when all the animals in a species die out and the species no longer exists

female animal that can become a mother when it grows up. Women and girls are female people.

government people who run a country and have the power to make important changes

habitat place where plants and animals grow and live. A forest is a kind of habitat.

herbivore animal that only eats plants

male animal that can become a father when it grows up. Men and boys are male people.

mammal animal that feeds its babies on the mother's milk and has some hair on its body

national park area of land where animals are protected and the habitat is looked after

species group of animals that can have babies together

traditional something which has been done in the same way for many years

WWF charity that helps endangered species. It is also called the World Wildlife Fund.

Index